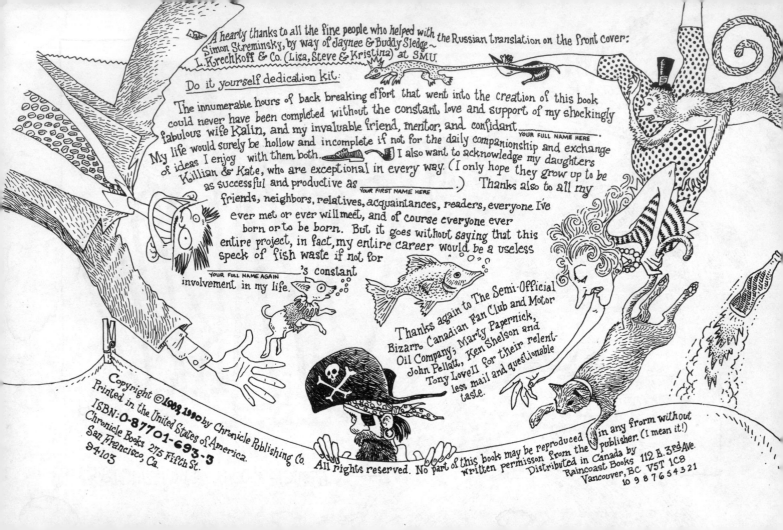

A hearty thanks to all the fine people who helped with the Russian translation on the front cover: Simon Streminsky, by way of Jaynee & Buddy Sledge~ L. Krechkoff & Co. (Lisa, Steve & Kristina) at SMU.

Do it yourself dedication kit:

The innumerable hours of back breaking effort that went into the creation of this book could never have been completed without the constant love and support of my shockingly fabulous wife Kalin, and my invaluable friend, mentor, and confidant _____. YOUR FULL NAME HERE My life would surely be hollow and incomplete if not for the daily companionship and exchange of ideas I enjoy with them both. I also want to acknowledge my daughters Killian & Kate, who are exceptional in every way. (I only hope they grow up to be as successful and productive as _____.) Thanks also to all my YOUR FIRST NAME HERE friends, neighbors, relatives, acquaintances, readers, everyone I've ever met or ever will meet, and of course everyone ever born or to be born. But it goes without saying that this entire project, in fact, my entire career would be a useless speck of fish waste if not for _____'s constant YOUR FULL NAME AGAIN involvement in my life.

Thanks again to The Semi-Official Bizarro Canadian Fan Club and Motor Oil Company; Marty Papernick, John Pellatt, Ken Shelson and Tony Lovell for their relentless mail and questionable taste.

Copyright © 1988, 1990 by Chronicle Publishing Co.
Printed in the United States of America.
ISBN: 0-87701-693-3
Chronicle Books 275 Fifth St.
San Francisco, Ca. 94103

Distributed in Canada by Raincoast Books 112 E. 3rd Ave.
Vancouver, BC V5T 1C8
10 9 8 7 6 5 4 3 2 1

3

START AT BACK OF BOOK
& FLIP THIS CORNER →
FORWARD WITH LEFT THUMB.

4

5

10

12

14

15

18

19

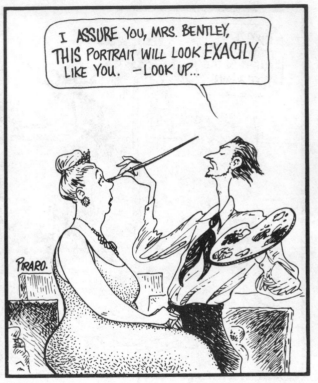

26

29

32

38

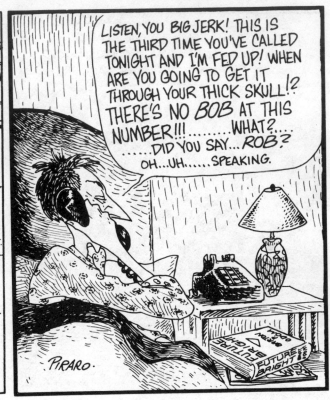

40

41

48

49

50

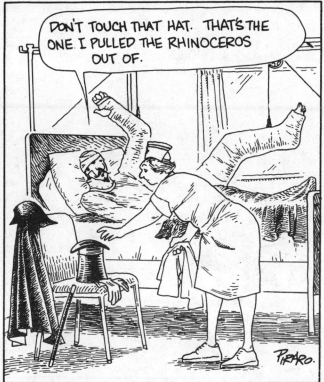

59

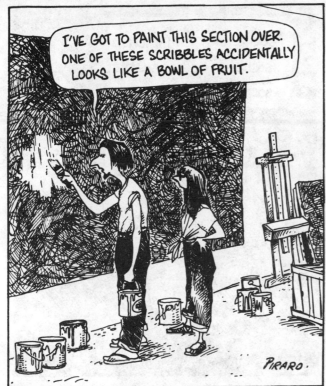

69

70

76

78

79

80

84

86

92

93

94

ABOUT THE AUTHOR'S PARENTS

Fred, of Sicilian descent, and Carol, of Irish, Scottish, and assorted other white folks descent were born in the Kansas City vicinity in the early to mid-twentieth century.

They spent their childhoods in varying degrees of bliss and agony, each completely unaware of the existence of the other. They met one day, under the seemingly unbearable pressure of adolescence, in the hallowed halls of the Kansas City Highschool for the Chronically Pleasant. Shortly thereafter they succumbed to that pressure, devised a plot to populate their immediate surroundings with small Catholics, and married.

Despite hectic careers as gameshow hosts, they managed to accomplish their goal with dizzying speed and moderate success (3 out of 4 still Catholic after 20 years.) Now nearing semi-retirement, they can often be seen enjoying a roller derby match on the front porch of their modest home in Tulsaslav, a suburb of Moscow. Neighbors report they can frequently be heard exalting their three beautiful daughters who reside comfortably within the boundaries of respectful society, and on occasion apologizing for their son, who draws pictures for a living.

The Piraros, 1971, counterclockwise from top right: Mom, Dad, Karen, Susan, Diane, Me.

START AT FRONT OF BOOK
← & FLIP THIS CORNER
FORWARD WITH RIGHT
THUMB AND LAUGH.